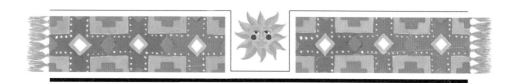

Fiesta!

Fiesta!

Mexico's Great Celebrations

Elizabeth Silverthorne

ILLUSTRATED BY JAN DAVEY ELLIS

THE MILLBROOK PRESS
BROOKFIELD, CONNECTICUT

HOUSTON PUBLIC LIBRARY

Special thanks to Carlos Najera,
Manager, Flores Branch,
Houston Public Library,
for his assistance with the
preparation of this book.

Library of Congress Cataloging-in-Publication Data
Silverthorne, Elizabeth, 1930–
Fiesta! : Mexico's great celebrations / by Elizabeth Silverthorne.
p.   cm.
Includes bibliographical references and index.
Summary: Describes the cultural and historical background and
ways of celebrating many religious and patriotic festivals of
Mexico. Includes instructions for making some of the traditional
crafts and foods.
ISBN 1-56294-055-4
1. Festivals—Mexico—Juvenile literature.   2. Mexico—Social
life and customs—Juvenile literature.   [1. Festivals—Mexico.
2. Mexico—Social life and customs.]   I. Title.
GT4814.A2S55   1992
394.2'6'0972—dc20   91-37178   CIP   AC

Contents

Introduction

Every day, somewhere in Mexico, people are sure to be enjoying a fiesta—a party or festival. Families hold fiestas to celebrate birthdays. Towns hold fiestas to honor a patron saint or a local hero. And many fiestas are celebrated all across the country. Some, like those at Christmas and Easter, are held for religious reasons. Others honor important people and events in Mexico's history.

Each fiesta is different. Often the celebration begins at dawn with the ringing of church bells or an explosion of fireworks. A fiesta may be simple or elaborate. It may last for a day or go on for a week or more. How long it lasts depends on why it is being celebrated and how much money the village or town has to spend on it.

Fiestas often include colorful parades or processions, music, dancing, spicy food, strong drinks, sports, bullfights, rodeos, and spectacular fireworks. Vendors arrive early on fiesta days to set up booths in the main plaza to sell toys and special souvenirs or food and drink. Balloons and bright tissue streamers attract buyers to the booths. Anyone with a few centavos (cents) can buy a paper mask and change into a clown, a princess, a bull, or a devil.

Groups of strolling musicians, called mariachi bands, may appear around any corner to serenade the crowd. There are also dancers in colorful costumes. All these will remain happy memories to brighten the lives of the watchers when they return to their everyday lives.

Visitors to Mexico enjoy the holiday atmosphere of fiestas. But they are sometimes bewildered by the number and variety of these celebrations. In this book you will find out why there are so many fiestas and what their importance is in the lives of the Mexican people. You will also find instructions for making some of the crafts and delicious foods that Mexican children enjoy at fiestas. But first, we need to learn a little about the land and the people of Mexico.

1

The Three Cultures

The enchanting country of Mexico lies just south of the United States like a great curved horn of plenty filled with color and contrast. High mountains wearing white caps of snow tower over vast stretches of desert where cacti reach their prickly limbs toward the scorching sun. Bright-green parrots and tiny jeweled hummingbirds dart through steamy rain forests. And people play on miles and miles of silvery beaches.

Overall, Mexico is about one fifth the size of the United States. If you could fly from one end of Mexico to the other in a helicopter, you would understand why no one can describe it without using the word *contrast.* Your main impression would be of a long, raised, flat central area, enclosed by mountain ranges that form a giant V around it. This Central Plateau is the heart of Mexico. Most of the big cities and many of the small farm towns are located here.

At the southern end of the Central Plateau lies Mexico City, the country's capital. The jagged mountains enclosing the plateau are the Sierra Madre. Notice that one arm of the Sierra Madre reaches up into Arizona and New Mexico.

The mountains of Mexico include many snowcapped extinct volcanoes and quite a few active ones. In 1943 a farmer in a village near Mexico City was amazed when a volcano suddenly popped up in his cornfield. It continued to grow, building a cone of lava and ash as it erupted and destroyed several villages.

Climate in Mexico is determined by altitude (height of the land above sea level), not by latitude (distance from the equator). Mexicans refer to the three main zones as the Tierra Caliente (hot land), the Tierra Templada (temperate land), and the Tierra Fría (cold land).

In the hot lands lie the steaming jungles and the coastal plains. In the mountains of the cold lands the temperature may remain below freezing throughout the year. Most of the country, however, does not have such extremes of temperature.

There is a saying that Mexico has only two seasons: the rainy season, from late May to late September, and the dry season, from October through April. But even in the rainy season, there is great contrast in the amount of rainfall in different regions. The annual rainfall varies from 2 to 4 inches (5 to 10 cm) in the deserts to 180 inches (450 cm) on the seaward slopes of the mountains.

The formal name for Mexico is Estados Unidos Mexicanos (United Mexican States). Like the United States, Mexico has a republican form of government with three branches—executive, legislative, and judicial. In Mexico, however, the president and the Congress have much more power than they do in the United States. The Mexican government has traditionally controlled the lives of the people by distributing land, regulating farm production, operating rural schools, providing health services, and running the railways and oil wells.

The culture of modern Mexico is basically a blend of the cultures of two very different peoples—the Indians and the

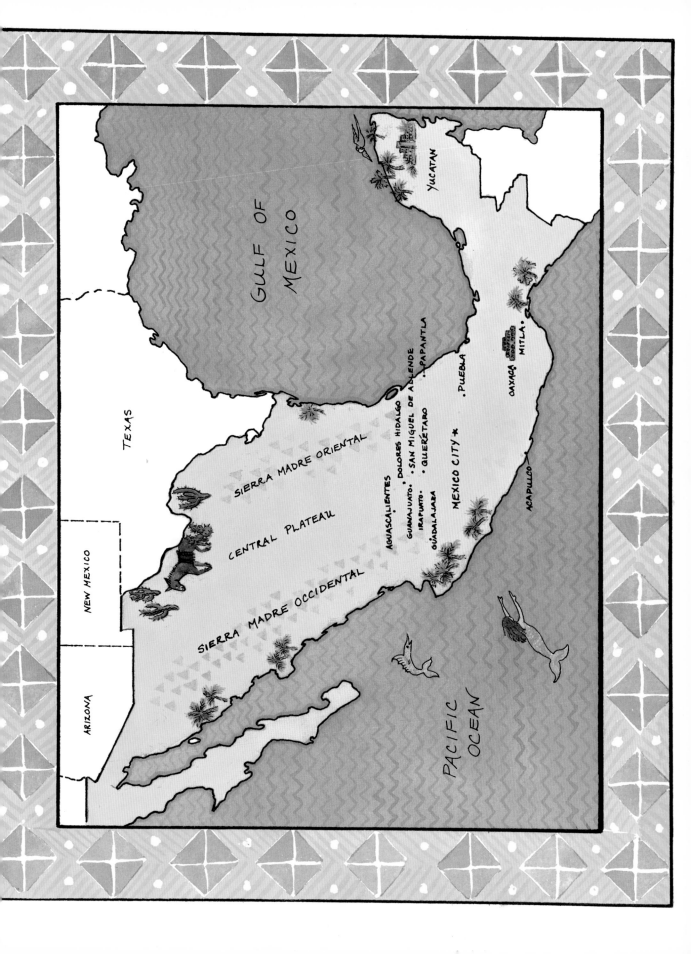

Spanish. We have to go very far back in time to see how each group helped make Mexico what it is today.

THE INDIANS In ancient times various Indian groups lived in Mexico. The Olmec and the Mayan peoples developed truly astonishing civilizations. They built huge buildings of beautifully carved stone. In addition to making fine pottery and carving jade jewelry, they were skillful painters and sculptors. They were also clever mathematicians and astronomers who made accurate calendars. And they used scientific methods to grow their crops. Today thousands of tourists each year visit the ruins of the Mayan fortresses and temples in the Yucatán Peninsula and marvel at their building skill.

In the ninth century, fierce Toltec tribes swooped down from northern Mexico into the central area. These invaders brought with them their religion, which included cruel sky and war gods who demanded human sacrifices. Other tribes opposed the Toltecs.

After several centuries of continuous warfare, the Aztecs emerged as the dominant civilization. Actually, they had borrowed many cultural elements from other groups, including many of their religious beliefs and myths.

The Aztecs, who called themselves Mexica, eventually gave the country and its citizens their names. Aztec legend says that the tribe was led to an island in Lake Texcoco by a message from a god. This god directed them to build their city where they found an eagle perched on a prickly-pear cactus holding a snake in its talons. Today the Mexican coat of arms displays this Aztec symbol of an eagle holding a snake. There is also a version of it in the center of the Mexican flag.

Religion guided the lives of the Aztecs. They worshipped many gods. In fact, almost everything in their lives had its separate god. There were numerous earth goddesses, gods of different crops, gods of various occupations such as water bearers and goldsmiths, and gods of the wind and of the morning star. They believed that all of their gods had to be honored and kept happy.

Above all, though, the Aztecs thought of themselves as "the People of the Sun." They believed they must give the sun god offerings of human blood and hearts. If they didn't do this, they feared he would disappear from the sky.

In addition to these ritual sacrifices, the Aztecs held many celebrations featuring pageants, flower offerings, and singing and dancing. Many of these ceremonies were performed in front of the temples that were built on top of tall pyramids. These temples can still be seen in Mexico.

THE SPANISH   About five hundred years ago, Spanish explorers began coming to Mexico from Europe. In 1519 the explorer Hernán Cortés and his followers entered the Valley of Mexico. There they saw the Aztec city of Tenochtitlán, where Mexico City is today. They were dazzled as they gazed on this widespread city with its grand temples and palaces, canals, and broad squares.

An Aztec legend told of the god Quetzalcoatl (the Plumed Serpent) who had sailed across the sea but who would one day return to rule his people. Quetzalcoatl was the god of learning and of the priesthood. One of the most important of all the gods, he was also called "the White God."

Therefore when the Indians saw the Spaniards with their strange white faces and plumed helmets, mounted on strange beasts (horses), they thought at first that Cortés might be the Plumed Serpent returning with his followers. So the Aztec emperor, Montezuma II, received him in his palace.

Soon, however, the Aztecs realized that Cortés was not their long-awaited god. It also became clear that the Spaniards were interested only in the Aztecs' treasures of gold and silver. The Aztecs revolted against the invaders. But in the uprising Montezuma was killed. After a number of uneven battles, the Spaniards with their iron weapons, guns, and horses defeated the Aztecs with their wooden bows and arrows and rawhide shields.

Spain ruled Mexico for the next three hundred years, from 1521 to 1821. This time is called the colonial period, the same name people in the United States use to identify the time that England ruled the American colonies. And just as part of what is now the United States was called New England (and still is called that, in fact), Spanish settlers called the country they emigrated to New Spain.

During the colonial period, the Spaniards used Indian laborers to build many splendid churches and cathedrals in Mexico. Even in very poor villages these buildings were so well built that some of them are still in use.

Spanish priests worked hard to convert the Mexican Indians to Christianity. At first, however, they did not have much success. Then the priests wisely allowed the Indians to keep many of their old ways of celebrating.

The Spanish priests actually found much beauty in the Aztec ceremonies (except for the horror of the human sacrifices). All the Indian children learned to dance, and hundreds of dancers performed in the elaborate temple services held in front of the great pyramids.

These services took place before a background of arches decorated with branches and flowers. All around were wooden cages filled with captive birds and animals. The dancers were mostly men and boys. They wore rich costumes made of feathers and ornaments of jade, pearls, turquoise, and obsidian. They also had jeweled masks. The massive gold breastplates of the warriors, along with their golden wristlets and anklets, flashed in the sun as they performed the intricate steps and movements of the dance.

Musicians performed on drums made of turtle shells or hollowed logs covered with skins, conch shells, and clay flutes. They also rubbed notched sticks or bones together to make music. The dancers carried rattles made of hollow gourds filled with pebbles.

As high-domed Spanish cathedrals replaced the Indian temples, religious fiestas were held in the churchyards. These spirited religious festivals were similar to the religious observances held in front of the pyramids, and the similarities helped in converting the Indians to the Catholic faith.

The greatest influence, however, came about quite naturally as the Spanish settlers and the native Indians began to marry one another and the races blended. And as their children had children, more and more became Christians. Today more than ninety percent of Mexicans are Roman Catholics. They call the pope, the leader of all Catholics, "El Papa."

THE MEXICANS Children born of a marriage of a Spaniard and an Indian were called mestizos. Today most Mexicans are mestizos (of mixed white and Indian ancestry). From ten to fifteen percent of Mexico's people are pure Indian (unmixed with white). Another small percent are pure white (unmixed with Indian).

Most Mexicans speak Spanish, the official language of the country. Indians, however, speak more than fifty dialects and languages. There are still groups of Indians in Mexico like the Huichols, who speak a dialect like that of the ancient Aztecs and practice their ancient religion.

God's Eye Ornament

These colorful woven wands may be carried for good luck or used as Christmas ornaments.

Equipment

two small wooden sticks or dowels (Popsicle sticks will do)
knitting yarn in two or three bright colors
scissors

How to make

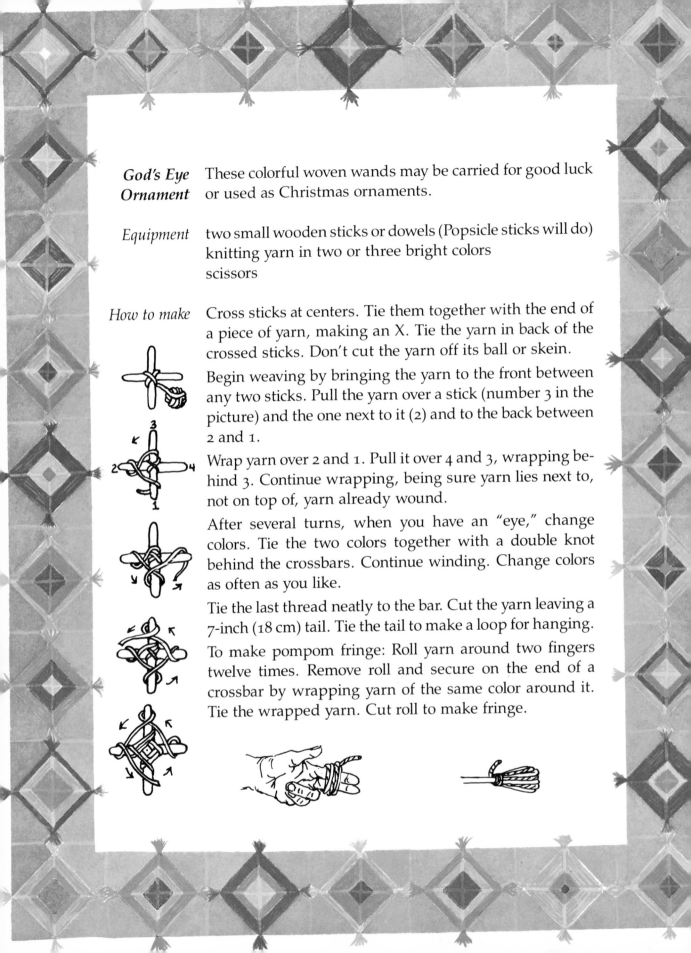

Cross sticks at centers. Tie them together with the end of a piece of yarn, making an X. Tie the yarn in back of the crossed sticks. Don't cut the yarn off its ball or skein.

Begin weaving by bringing the yarn to the front between any two sticks. Pull the yarn over a stick (number 3 in the picture) and the one next to it (2) and to the back between 2 and 1.

Wrap yarn over 2 and 1. Pull it over 4 and 3, wrapping behind 3. Continue wrapping, being sure yarn lies next to, not on top of, yarn already wound.

After several turns, when you have an "eye," change colors. Tie the two colors together with a double knot behind the crossbars. Continue winding. Change colors as often as you like.

Tie the last thread neatly to the bar. Cut the yarn leaving a 7-inch (18 cm) tail. Tie the tail to make a loop for hanging.

To make pompom fringe: Roll yarn around two fingers twelve times. Remove roll and secure on the end of a crossbar by wrapping yarn of the same color around it. Tie the wrapped yarn. Cut roll to make fringe.

The Huichols live in remote, roadless areas in the Sierra Madre. They have kept their old ways and resisted change. In their temples, they perform their traditional dances and make offerings to honor Our Father Sun, Grandfather Fire, and other gods and goddesses.

One of their offerings has been adopted by outsiders. This is the "God's Eye" ornament. It is made by weaving colored yarn in a diamond pattern over crossed sticks. It is a popular item for vendors to sell at fiestas and is often used as a decoration on Christmas trees.

Just as American colonies rebelled against their mother country, England, and won their freedom, the Mexican colony of New Spain rebelled against its mother country, Spain. The revolt began in 1810. It took eleven years and cost many lives. The rebels won their independence in 1821, and the United Mexican States came into being.

Near the center of Mexico City there is a plaza where you can see symbols of the three cultures that have shaped Mexico. It is called La Plaza de Tres Culturas (The Plaza of Three Cultures). On one side of it are the ruins of an ancient Aztec pyramid. On the other side stands a weathered gray Spanish colonial church. And in the background modern steel and glass buildings loom over both.

Just as there are great contrasts in the geography and climate of Mexico, there are great contrasts in the people who live there today. Some of the people are very rich, but others are very poor.

There is one thing that all Mexicans have in common, though. Whether rich or poor, young or old, they all enjoy fiestas. In the following chapters we will explore these fiestas in all their color and variety.

Religious Fiestas

Religious festivals still center around the church or cathedral. In most Mexican towns the church is located conveniently next to the *zócalo*, or main plaza. Modern Mexicans spend hours building archways of flowers and leaves around church entranceways and decorating their churches with colored tissue paper and flowers. This is very like the way the Indians of ancient times decorated their temples.

Traces of the older Indian culture can also be seen today in the most solemn church celebrations. Many of the dances performed at religious fiestas, especially those featuring animals and birds, go back to pagan times. Instead of the fires that were lit to honor the old gods, candles are lit to honor Catholic saints.

In addition, the skillful craftsmanship that has been handed down through the generations can be seen in the beautiful artwork at festivals. Huge candles that look as though they were made of lace are carried in parades behind the statues of saints. Metallic paper is cut and hammered into intricate designs and hung outside the churches. Colorful flowers and birds made of tissue paper decorate the plazas.

All year round the Mexican religious calendar is crowded with fiestas, as every village honors its own patron saint. Some towns hold more than six religious fiestas a year. However, the most important religious holiday for Mexicans is on December 12. This is the feast day of their national patron saint, the Virgin of Guadalupe.

THE VIRGIN OF GUADALUPE

According to legend, an Indian named Juan Diego had a vision of the Virgin Mary while he was gathering herbs on a hill near Mexico City in 1531, ten years after the Spanish conquest. She told him to go to the bishop and have him build a shrine to her at the place where he had the vision. But the bishop would not listen to Juan Diego, telling him he was crazy.

Three days later the Virgin again appeared to Juan. This time she told him to go to a barren hillside and pick the roses that he would find there. Juan knew that only cacti ever grew on that stony slope. Still, he obeyed the Virgin. He was amazed to find that roses were indeed growing on the hill.

Juan Diego gathered the roses and took them to the Virgin. She wrapped the roses in his cloak, or serape, and sent him to the bishop who had refused to build a shrine in her honor. When Juan opened his cloak, the roses disappeared and a picture of the Virgin appeared on the cloak. The bishop declared that it was a miracle and built the church to honor the Virgin. She then became the patron saint of Mexico.

In many villages, celebrations begin the week before December 12. Children visit their local churches on the Day of the Virgin of Guadalupe. Little boys dress up as *Dieguitos* in memory of Juan Diego. They wear serapes, sandals, and painted mustaches.

[19]

There are Guadalupe churches in many towns in Mexico. But many people try to visit the original church site, outside Mexico City. There, at the Basilica of Our Lady of Guadalupe, they can view the miraculous cloak, which is enshrined in its own altar. They can also take part in the festival. Some travel on foot or on burros for days, and some arrive in limousines. Young and old, rich and poor bring gifts for the Virgin.

A huge fair is held during the fiesta. *Conchero* dancers entertain the crowd. These dance groups travel from fiesta to fiesta, dancing to the music of guitars or lutes made from the shells (*conchas*) of armadillos. The *conchero* dancers preserve the ancient dances of their ancestors in the central highlands of Mexico. Their colorful costumes include tall plumed headdresses, wide capes, sequined robes, embroidered shields, and clusters of bells and dried shells on their ankles. They dance for hours and seem never to get tired.

Also very popular at this festival are the *matachin* sword dancers. They are a group dedicated to the service, through dancing, of the Virgin of Guadalupe. The dancers wear tall pointed headdresses. Their faces are partly covered by fringes, and their costumes include aprons and brightly colored ribbons. In one hand each dancer carries a gourd rattle, and in the other a gaily painted wooden sword.

There are twelve dances in a set. Some of these are "The Battle," "The Cross," "The Procession," and "The Braids" (a maypole dance). In "The Cross," two lines of matachines exchange places in a crisscross movement. Several of the dances feature *malinches*, young boys dressed up as girls. They are named after an Aztec girl who was an interpreter for Cortés.

The last dance in the set is a humorous one, "El Toro" ("The Bull"). The dancers make a circle like a bullring, and the bull acts like a clown. *El Abuelo* (the Grandfather) is another clownish character that appears in the dance. The dance ends with the pretended killing of the bull.

Food booths and pushcarts offer refreshments at the fiesta. Tortillas are popular. Corn tortillas are to the people of Mexico what bread is to the people of the United States. Tortillas are flat, pancakelike rounds made from corn (or maize).

Tortillas are mixed with many other foods. They are the basis for tacos, *chalupas*, enchiladas, and tostadas. Tacos are tortillas filled with chopped meat, cheese, or chicken. *Chalupas* are crisply fried tortillas piled with beans, tomatoes, shredded lettuce, and grated cheese. Enchiladas are soft, rolled tortillas stuffed with ground meat or chicken, covered with a hot, spicy tomato sauce.

Tostadas are tortillas fried in deep fat until they are crisp. They are used as spoons to eat rice and *frijoles refritos* (beans that have been cooked, mashed, and fried). In addition, tamales are sure to star at any fiesta. They are made by spread-

Tacos

The Mexicans eat tacos just as people eat hamburgers and hot dogs in the United States.

Ingredients
- 1 pound (450 g) ground chicken or hamburger
- 1 teaspoon (5 ml) premixed Mexican seasoning
- 1 teaspoon (5 ml) onion flakes
- 1/2 teaspoon (2.5 ml) dried cilantro (coriander)
- 1/4 teaspoon (1.25 ml) cumin
  - dash of cayenne
  - taco shells (box of 12)
- 12 ounces (340 g) shredded cheese (cheddar or Monterey Jack)
- 2 tomatoes
- 1 avocado
- 1 small head of lettuce

Equipment
medium skillet with lid
chopping board
chopping knife
mixing spoon
measuring spoons

How to make
Brown meat in skillet. Add premixed Mexican seasoning, onion flakes, cilantro, cumin, and cayenne. Simmer covered for about an hour. Stir occasionally.

While meat is simmering, dice the tomatoes and avocado. Shred the lettuce. Fill taco shells with the meat mixture. Top with tomatoes, avocado, lettuce, and cheese.

This recipe makes twelve tacos.

ing seasoned pork, beef, or chicken over a coarse cornmeal dough. This is then wrapped in cornhusks and steamed. Children especially enjoy the booths that offer sweets such as *polvorones* (sugar cookies) and *buñuelos* (a kind of doughnut).

CHRISTMAS Hardly have the celebrations of the Day of the Virgin of Guadalupe ended when the Christmas season begins. In Mexico it is celebrated from December 16 through January 6. Streets, buildings, plazas, and lawns are decorated. Inside the homes there may be Christmas trees. But the *Nacimiento* (manger scene) is more important to Catholic families in Mexico.

Each manger scene is different. The figures are made of painted wood or clay. They are carefully placed against backgrounds of straw or Spanish moss. Some of these treasured figures have been handed down for generations. New figures are added over the years.

The scenes may grow to take up half a room and reach from floor to ceiling. They are decorated with paper flowers, tinsel, ornaments, wreaths, and figures of various animals and people besides the Holy Family. Some scenes even include Santa Claus and his reindeer. On Christmas Eve the tiny figure of *El Niño Dios* (Baby God) is placed in the manger.

Beginning on December 16 and for the next nine days, through December 24, *Posada* (inn or shelter) processions reenact the search of Mary and Joseph for lodging. In many towns the *Posada* is performed by children who carry lanterns and platforms with figures of Mary and Joseph. Sometimes a girl dressed as Mary rides on a real donkey and a boy who represents Joseph walks along beside her.

Stopping at the home of a neighbor, they beg to be taken in, singing, "I am tired. I beg for rest." The children who are inside behind the door sing, "Go away, go away, there is no room." The procession goes from house to house until at last they reach a house where they are admitted. Then, after prayers around the manger, it is time for the social part of the evening.

Refreshments are served, and there is a piñata to add to the fun. Piñatas are made of clay or papier-mâché (paper pulp mixed with paste). They are covered with curls of brightly colored crepe or tissue paper. Piñatas may be any size or shape. At Christmastime, stars, birds, lambs and other traditional animal forms are popular. But today Santa Claus, Mickey Mouse, and satellite piñatas are often seen.

The piñata is hung from the ceiling of a room or porch or from a tree limb in the courtyard. It has a rope attached so it can be pulled up and down. Beginning with the youngest child, the players are blindfolded and twirled around. Each player is given several chances to break the piñata with a stick. Someone jerks the rope to move the piñata up and down and sideways.

The blindfolded player swings wildly at the moving target, as the other players yell, "Higher!" "Lower!" "Harder!" Finally someone gives the piñata a lucky whack and breaks it. Everyone scrambles for the candy, small toys, and good-luck charms that shower down.

Special events are featured in regional celebrations, such as those in Oaxaca and Querétaro. Each church in Oaxaca presents a procession called a *calenda* on Christmas Eve. Members of the congregations of about thirty churches work together to build the floats for the *calenda*. Everyone, young and old, does whatever he can to make decorations or costumes to make their float beautiful.

Querétaro also has an impressive parade of floats on Christmas Eve. But more visitors go there to see the dazzling fireworks display. A special fireworks structure called a *castillo* (castle) is seen at almost any good-sized fiesta. But the ones at Querétaro at Christmas are especially grand.

The light bamboo frame of the huge *castillo* is built in stages on the plaza. Each of the stories is loaded with sparklers, pinwheels, rockets, and strings of firecrackers. As each stage goes off in succession, there is a cascade of light and color and explosions of sound.

The Christmas season ends on January 6, Twelfth Night. This is the Día de los Tres Reyes (Day of the Three Kings). It honors the Three Kings (or Wise Men, or Magi) who traveled from the East on camels following a bright star to the stable where Jesus was born in Bethlehem.

The Three Kings brought rich gifts to the baby Jesus, and children in Mexico believe the trio also brings them gifts on January 6. The children leave their shoes near a door or a window or by the manger scene. They also put out water for the weary camels. In the morning the water is gone and the shoes are filled with gifts.

Today many Mexican homes also have evergreen Christmas trees with colored lights, and Santa Claus brings Christmas gifts on December 25. In this way, lucky children receive gifts on both Christmas Day and on the Day of the Three Kings.

On January 6 many parties and family celebrations feature a special cake called the Three Kings' Cake. It is baked in the shape of a crown and studded with bits of candied cherries and pineapple that look like jewels. A tiny doll is baked inside the cake. It is supposed to bring good luck to the person who finds it.

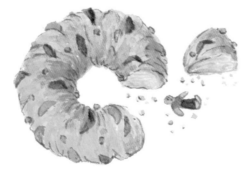

Piñatas A quick and easy way to make a piñata is to put two or three large paper sacks inside one another. Fill with candy, toys, gum. Fold the ends over and staple or tape together. Decorate with paint, construction paper, and tissue paper ruffles.

A good sturdy piñata can be made using a big balloon and papier-mâché. This is how to make a star piñata:

Equipment large round balloon, inflated and tied
newspaper cut into strips 1 to 2 inches (3 to 5 cm) wide
flour and water paste (one part flour to two parts water)
eight sheets tissue paper, each 20 by 30 inches (50 by 75 cm), in three colors, such as white, blue, and magenta
newspapers
masking tape
rubber cement
10 feet (3 m) heavy twine

How to make the piñata Dip newspaper strips in paste and apply four layers to balloon. Leave 3 inches (8 cm) at stem end of balloon for opening.

Paste five cones (see directions following) onto wet piñata.

Let form dry completely. Deflate balloon by snipping a hole in the exposed end.

Attach twine, circling the piñata from top to bottom in several loops. Use masking tape to hold twine in place. Make a stout loop at the top.

Decorate the piñata with tissue paper ruffles (see directions following). Use white for the cones, and another color for the piñata form. Glue the ruffles on in rows with rubber cement.

Make tassels by cutting one sheet of white tissue and one of colored tissue into strips ¼ inch (6 mm) wide. Divide the strips into five equal bunches of mixed colored and white tissue. Glue or staple one bunch to each cone tip.

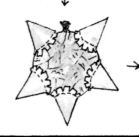 → 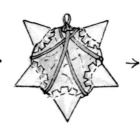 →  →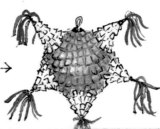

How to make the ruffles	Take a sheet of tissue paper, folded as it comes from the package, and cut lengthwise down the middle to make two strips, each about 3 inches (8 cm) wide.

How to make the ruffles

Take a sheet of tissue paper, folded as it comes from the package, and cut lengthwise down the middle to make two strips, each about 3 inches (8 cm) wide.

Cut slashes every ⅛ inch (3 mm) along the folded edge of each strip, extending to within ½ inch (1 cm) of cut edge.

Unfold strip and refold to reverse side. Glue edges together.

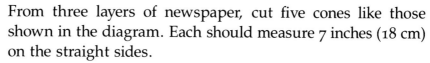

How to make the cones

From three layers of newspaper, cut five cones like those shown in the diagram. Each should measure 7 inches (18 cm) on the straight sides.

Form the cones by overlapping the straight edges and cementing them together.

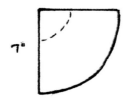

Make cuts 1 inch (3 cm) deep around the base of each cone. Fold the cut edges back and paste them onto the piñata.

For a fancy touch, tip the cones with shiny aluminum foil. Cut five tips like those in the diagram, each 3 inches (8 cm) on the straight sides. Fasten the tips to the ends of the cones with rubber cement.

THE EASTER SEASON The celebrations connected with Easter, like those connected with Christmas, stretch out over many weeks. Carnival happens in February or March during the week before Lent. (Lent begins on Ash Wednesday, which is a movable feast on the church calendar. That is, the date varies from year to year.)

Being in Mexico during Carnival is like being in the middle of a brilliant, fast-moving dream. There are constant surprises as strolling mariachi bands spring up everywhere. Fireworks explode at all hours of the day and night. And characters in fantastic costumes pop out of doorways and from around corners at every turn.

The more organized merrymaking at Carnival includes lavish masquerade dances and battles of flowers, in which beautifully dressed women and children pelt each other and bystanders with blossoms and petals. Carnival queens are elected, and there are parades of gaily decorated floats and marchers in gorgeous costumes. Children ride on many of the floats or march along in the parades.

Children also especially enjoy the custom of egg smashing. Eggs are blown out, painted in bright colors, and filled with confetti. In the Battle of the Eggs, boys and girls form two lines. At a signal from the leader they begin to walk past each other. They try to break their eggs on each other's heads as they pass.

Carnival is not a religious festival in itself. But it is directly related to Lent, which is one of the most important seasons of the Church. In Mexico, the forty days of Lent are not gloomy as they are in some Catholic countries. Various regions hold individual festivals. Many people make pilgrimages to shrines where miracles are said to have happened. In some areas there are fairs, performances by dance troupes, cockfights and bullfights, flower festivals, and fireworks.

On Palm Sunday, at the beginning of Holy Week, there is a blessing of palm branches in churches throughout Mexico.

Week-long fiestas sponsored by the churches follow. On Maundy Thursday and Good Friday there are passion plays that tell the story of Christ's Crucifixion. And in some towns there are processions that reenact the story of Christ's journey as he carried the cross on which he was crucified.

Holy Saturday, the day before Easter Sunday, is an exciting time, especially for children. Ugly papier-mâché figures of Judas, the disciple who betrayed Jesus, are made in homes or bought in markets. Adults sometimes pretend the figures are local politicians they don't like. The Judas figure is hung from a streetlamp, a balcony, or some other elevation. Small toys, candies, and firecrackers are tied to the figure.

At 10 A.M. on Holy Saturday, church bells ring, children shake rattles, and the first string of firecrackers on the Judas figure is lighted. It explodes with a series of loud bangs and in turn sets off other strings of crackers. When the Judas figure catches fire, the attached gifts and goodies fall. There is much shouting and laughing as everyone tries to catch something.

Strict regulations about fireworks in some cities have limited these traditional Judases. Instead, sometimes the Judas piñata is beaten vigorously with sticks until it breaks, scattering candies and goodies for the children.

Easter Sunday is a time for church ceremonies and joyful music to celebrate Christ's rising from the tomb. Village fiestas include singing, dancing, feasting, and fireworks displays.

OTHER RELIGIOUS FIESTAS Besides the three important fiestas of the Virgin of Guadalupe, Christmas, and Easter, Mexicans celebrate many other religious fiestas through the year.

On January 17, St. Anthony's Day, Mexican children put ribbons and flower garlands on their pets. They then take them to their local church to be blessed by the priest. St. Anthony the Abbot founded the first Christian monastery. He was also known for his love of children and animals.

St. Anthony's Day is therefore a fiesta for giving attention to children and animals. In addition to cats and dogs, calves and ponies, and sheep and goats, the children bring birds in cages, turtles in boxes, and fish in jugs of water to be blessed.

On February 2 all of Mexico celebrates the Day of Our Lady of La Candelaria (Candlemas). On this day, candles and seeds for planting are blessed in churches. Many towns hold parades, dances, and bullfights at the time of this fiesta. In some towns there is a "running of the bulls." During this, bulls are turned loose in the streets to let young boys who dream of becoming bullfighters practice confronting them.

Early in June, the festival of Corpus Christi is celebrated in Mexico. Children in traditional costumes bring fruits and vegetables and sometimes live birds to their parish churches as token offerings of the first fruits of the harvest.

In colonial days this was the day people came to their churches to pay their tithes (church taxes). Many of them rode mules, which they hitched outside the church. Today at Corpus Christi fiestas, toy mules with their *panniers* (baskets) filled with fruit or flowers are sold in the Cathedral in Mexico City and in churches elsewhere in Mexico. At markets, vendors feature folk toys of *mulitos* (little mules) made of palm, rushes, straw, wood, or dried cornhusks.

One of the most amazing sights in Mexico can be seen on Corpus Christi Day in Papantla in the state of Veracruz. It is here on this day that the famous *voladores* (flying dancers) perform their dangerous aerial dance. Five slender Indians climb a tall pole nearly 100 feet (30 meters) high that has been placed in front of an ancient pyramid.

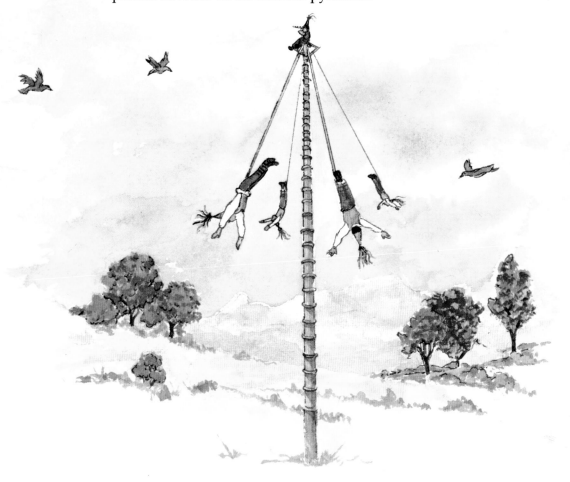

The leader of the group remains at the very top of the pole on a small platform. He plays a drum or sometimes a flute as he slowly turns around. Meanwhile, the other performers tie ropes around their bodies. At a signal from the leader, the performers fling themselves outward and fly around the pole upside down as the ropes unwind. Like birds, they fly in larger and larger circles, each making thirteen turns as the watchers gasp.

Just before it appears they will crash into the ground, they somersault lightly to their feet. The flight of these "birdmen" is an example of how an ancient Indian ceremony in honor of the sun has become part of a Christian holy day.

The Feast of Saint John on June 24 is also called "bath day." In rural areas people bathe in rivers in memory of Saint John the Baptist, who baptized people, including Jesus, in a river. Bath day is a time for lighthearted fun. Anywhere in Mexico unsuspecting victims may get a surprise bath by having a bucket of water thrown on them or by being pushed into a fountain or a swimming pool.

Even the dead have a fiesta in Mexico. For Mexicans, death is a part of life. It is not something to be quickly covered over or hidden. In ancient times the Indians held a month-long festival of Death and Flowers as a reminder of the beauty and fleeting nature of life. The last day of their celebration fell on November 1. This was the same day as the Spanish festival called All Souls' Day, when the spirits of the dead were thought to return to earth.

Today in Mexico *El Día de los Muertos*, the Day of the Dead, begins on October 31 and lasts through November 2. Weeks before the fiesta, markets are filled with toys related to death—cardboard skeletons that dance on strings, clay skulls, coffins with skeletons that pop out of them. Families make careful preparations for the fiesta. They sweep and clean

graves and tombstones. In their homes they set up altars with pictures of dead family members. Around these altars they place candles, flowers, and incense. The favorite foods of the dead are also placed near the altars.

Bakeries feature a special round cake called *pan de los muertos.* It may be decorated with different icings in the shape of a skull and crossbones. Sometimes the bread is baked in the shape of a man or a woman or a child to represent someone who has died. Children happily eat small blue and pink candy skulls that have their names pasted on the foreheads.

The Day of the Dead is a time to watch processions of marchers in skeleton masks and other costumes representing death. Sometimes groups of young men carry coffins from which fake skeletons pop up and wave playfully to the crowd. It is also a time to visit churches and pray for the dead.

Above all, the Day of the Dead is a time for families to visit cemeteries. They bring candles and food and armloads of *caléndulas* (marigolds), the special flower of the dead. They pile flowers over and around the freshly cleaned graves of loved ones. Petals are pulled off the marigolds and spread on the tombs in the form of crosses.

Families have picnics in the cemeteries. At night, hundreds of candles glow as families keep watch beside the decorated graves. Soft music from a mariachi band serenading the spirits of the dead may be heard in the background.

Although the Day of the Dead is a time to remember those who have gone, it is not an unhappy fiesta. Rather it is a time to connect the past and the future with the present. And it reassures those who are living that when they too have died, they will not be forgotten.

Patriotic Fiestas

Viva Mexico! In addition to religious fiestas, Mexicans hold festivals year-round to honor important dates in Mexico's history or to mark the birthdays of famous Mexican leaders. Like religious festivals, these include bands, fireworks, fairs, dancing, and village sports such as bull-baiting and horse racing. Plus, there is always lots of good food and drink.

Instead of religious processions and church services, patriotic fiestas feature parades, speeches, and modern sports events. On these holidays, Mexicans may wear national costumes. The one named after the *China Poblana* (the Chinese Girl of Puebla) is one of the best known.

Legend says that the *China Poblana* was a princess of Delhi in India. Pirates kidnapped her and brought her as a slave to Mexico in the 1600s. She was bought as a servant by a wealthy man and his wife in Puebla. After they died, she married a Chinese man. She became a Christian and was known far and wide for her piety and good deeds.

Her favorite costume consisted of a full red and green skirt decorated with sequins and beads, an embroidered short-sleeved white blouse, and a silk shawl. This costume was adopted by Mexican women and came to be known as the *china poblana*.

February 5, Constitution Day, is a national holiday with parades and flag displays to commemorate the constitutions of 1857 and 1917. The Constitution of 1857 is an important landmark in Mexico's history. But it was fiercely opposed by military and religious groups because it took away many of their privileges. Only after a bloody civil war, called the War of the Reform, was this constitution accepted. It called for freedom of the press, religion, and education along with many other democratic reforms.

The Constitution of 1917 revised and updated the provisions of the 1857 constitution. It had the idealistic goal of improving the lives of working people by providing for an eight-hour workday and a minimum wage. It also sought to provide health and welfare programs and better education. No wonder Mexicans hold festivals to mark Constitution Day, even if they are still struggling to achieve some of the reforms these documents set out.

Mexico celebrates Flag Day on February 24. Like Flag Day in the United States (June 14), it is a time for people to display flags on their homes and on public buildings. It is also a time for patriotic parades and speeches. The speakers often remind the people that the Mexican flag came into being after Mexico won its freedom from Spain in 1821.

In 1934 the flag was adopted in its present form. Next to the staff, on the left, the vertical green stripe stands for independence. The vertical white stripe in the middle bears a version of the coat of arms. And the red stripe on the right represents union.

The coat of arms on the flag shows an eagle with a snake in its beak and talons, standing on a prickly-pear cactus. As we have seen, this symbol is a reminder of the legend that says Mexico City (originally the Aztec city of Tenochtitlán) was built by Indians on a spot where they saw an eagle with a snake in its beak standing on a cactus.

Mexican Flag

You can make this flag from construction paper, different-colored fabrics, or with white paper by tracing and coloring it. The staff can be gold or brown. The left band is green for independence. The middle band is white for religion. The right band is red for union. The cactus and the garland are green, and so is the snake. The eagle is dark brown with black markings.

BENITO JUÁREZ All of Mexico celebrates the birthday of its national hero, Benito Juárez, on March 21. He is often called the "Abraham Lincoln of Mexico" because of his legendary honesty and his deep devotion to his country. Born in the state of Oaxaca in 1806, Juárez was a full-blooded Indian. Orphaned at the age of three, he rose from working as a houseboy to become a law student.

Juárez went on to hold various government posts, including governor of his state. In 1861 he became president of Mexico—the first Indian to hold that post. Like Lincoln, he dressed in a simple black suit and cape and wore a black stovepipe hat. And like Lincoln he was loved by the common people. He played a leading role in framing the Constitution of 1857.

However, his reforms (called La Reforma) were resented by the church and by big landowners, who asked Emperor Napoleon III of France for help. The emperor sent Archduke Maximilian of Austria with a French army to establish a rule in Mexico. Juárez and his followers met the French army at Puebla and won a temporary victory on May 5, 1862. The French, however, succeeded in driving Juárez out of Mexico. Under pressure from the United States, France began to withdraw its army. Maximilian was executed. Juárez returned to the presidency and remained in office until his death in 1872.

On his birthday, Mexicans recall La Reforma and all that Juárez did for them. He is credited with separating church and state, establishing religious tolerance, freeing the Indians from bondage, and changing the land system. (After the Spanish conquered Mexico in 1521, they took most of the land away from the Indians and set up large estates called *haciendas*. The Indians worked on these almost as slaves.) On March 21 posters with Juárez's picture on them spring up all over Mexico. Because of his humble beginnings and his ancestry, his birthday also is celebrated as the Day of the Indian Child.

CINCO DE MAYO May 5, Cinco de Mayo, commemorates the day that Juárez led his ragtag followers to victory against the well-trained French invaders at Puebla. It is one of the most important fiesta days in Mexico. Many towns and cities mark the holiday with grand parades, mock battles, dances, and fireworks. Flower festivals are popular, with everything from floats to people decorated with brightly colored flowers, both paper and real.

Parades usually start moving about eleven o'clock, when the first band strikes up a lively marching tune. Marchers dressed as French and Mexican generals lead the way. Soldiers follow, armed like the original freedom fighters with machetes and old-fashioned rifles. Paraders wearing skirts and flowery hats represent the women who traveled with the army to cook and care for the men. It's easy to recognize those portraying French soldiers. They are the ones carrying knapsacks with wine bottles sticking out of them.

At mid-afternoon the "battle" begins in the plaza. Rifles and cannon roar, and there is much smoke and shouting. At nightfall the Mexican and French generals meet face-to-face for a sword battle. The Mexican general, of course, wins. A gigantic fireworks display ends the celebration.

INDEPENDENCE DAY Although Cinco de Mayo is very important to Mexicans, Diez y Seis de Septiembre, September 16, is even more so. This is their Independence Day, a national birthday. On this date Mexicans remember the beginning of the revolution against Spain. There are fiestas all across the country, with the biggest one in Mexico City. The hero of this day is Father Miguel Hidalgo y Costilla, called "the Father of Mexican Independence."

In the early years of the nineteenth century, the people of New Spain became increasingly restless under Spanish rule. They also became inspired by the success of the American and

Chicken Enchiladas

Enchiladas are as popular as tacos in Mexico. But while tacos are crisp and crunchy, enchiladas are soft and chewy.

Ingredients
- 1 pound (450 g) cooked and shredded chicken
- ²/₃ cup (160 ml) sour cream
- ²/₃ cup (160 ml) canned or bottled salsa
- 8 ounces (225 g) shredded cheddar cheese
- 8 tortillas
- 1 teaspoon (5 ml) oil (for greasing baking dish)

Equipment
measuring cup
measuring spoons
large baking dish (9×13 inches)

How to make
Preheat the oven to 350° F (175° C). Grease baking dish with teaspoon of oil. Place an equal amount of chicken in the middle of each tortilla. Top with 1 teaspoon (15 ml) sour cream. Fold up both sides of the tortilla tightly. Place the enchiladas seam side down in the baking dish. Cover with salsa and cheese. Bake for fifteen to twenty minutes. Top with the rest of the sour cream before serving. This recipe makes eight enchiladas.

French revolutions. Groups therefore began to hold secret meetings to discuss how they could throw off the harsh rule of far-off Spain. The leader of one of these groups was Father Hidalgo, a kindhearted priest in the little town of Dolores (about 150 miles, or 240 kilometers, north of Mexico City).

Father Hidalgo helped plan a revolt for late fall of 1810. He and his officers realized that time was needed to make swords and bullets and to train the Indians in fighting skills. But the Spanish authorities found out about the uprising. Two months before the planned revolt, Father Hidalgo learned that orders had been given for the arrest of all the leaders of his group. There was no time for further preparations.

At eleven o'clock on the night of September 15, 1810, Father Hidalgo rang the church bell in Dolores, as if to call his congregation to Mass. When the people gathered, he rallied them to action with the cries that have rung down through the years. *"Viva Mexico! Viva la independencia!"* he shouted. And the excited crowd echoed back each cry.

Criollos (wealthy Mexicans of Spanish blood), mestizos, and Indians united with Father Hidalgo. Some of the ragged army had ancient guns. But many of them had only clubs, knives, or stone slings as they began the march to Mexico City.

A terrible battle took place in Guanajuato between Spanish soldiers and Hidalgo's followers. The Indian and mestizo army sacked the town and killed the Spaniards. The cobblestone streets flowed with blood before Father Hidalgo and his officers could bring order out of the chaos.

The rebels captured other cities and marched on to the outskirts of Mexico City. But at the gates of the capital they hesitated, and some of the rebels deserted the army. The fighting continued in other places, but within a year Father Hidalgo was captured and executed.

However, there were others to take up the cause. Father Hidalgo's *Grito de Dolores* (Cry of Dolores) became the battle cry of the Mexican War of Independence, and eleven years later the people of Mexico did achieve their freedom.

Today in Mexico on September 15, the eve of Independence Day, crowds gather in the *zócalos* of cities and towns and villages. The huge square in Mexico City is decorated with flags and flowers and lit with thousands of red, green, and white lights. Vendors selling whistles, horns, papier-mâché helmets, confetti, and toys painted in red, white, and green do a good business.

This is the spot where the Aztec emperor Montezuma II had his palace and where the conquering Spaniards built the great palace that still stands. Here women in *rebozos* (long scarves) and men in serapes (cloaks) mix with those wearing styles from the United States. Mariachi musicians dressed in tight-fitting suits trimmed with silver buttons and decorated wide-brimmed hats entertain the crowd. There are also some marimba (xylophone) players.

As always, plenty of food is available. In one place is a stand with slices of fruit artistically arranged. In other places are booths selling spicy tamales and tacos and candies. Still others satisfy thirst with colorful *refrescos* (fruit drinks) or delicious hot chocolate.

Everyone keeps an eye on the clock. As it begins to strike eleven, silence falls. On the last stroke the president of Mexico steps out onto the palace balcony overlooking the *zócalo*. He rings the historic liberty bell that called Father Hidalgo's followers to revolt. At the last stroke of the hour, he gives the *Grito de Dolores.*

"*Viva la independencia*" and "*Viva Mexico,*" he shouts, and the crowd echoes back the cry. At the same time all across Mexico,

Mexican Hot Chocolate

The people of Mexico have been drinking hot chocolate since the days of the ancient Aztecs. If you make some, it will help you capture the flavor of a Mexican fiesta.

In a large supermarket or a Mexican specialty store, you can find Mexican chocolate already sweetened and flavored with cinnamon. Put a square or round of chocolate in a cup of hot milk. After the chocolate melts, pour mixture in a pitcher and beat with wooden beater (*molinillo*) or wire whip until frothy.

Regular chocolate or cocoa may be substituted for Mexican chocolate by adding sugar and cinnamon to taste.

Polvorones

You'll always find some treat like these Mexican sugar cookies at a fiesta to satisfy your sweet tooth.

Ingredients

- 2 cups (480 ml) flour
- ¾ cup (180 ml) sugar
- ½ teaspoon (2.5 ml) cinnamon
- 1 cup (240 ml) soft butter or margarine
  - extra sugar and cinnamon

Equipment

flour sifter
electric beater
measuring spoon
mixing bowl
cookie sheet

How to make

Preheat oven to 300° F (150° C). Sift flour, cinnamon, and sugar together. Cream butter with beater. Then gradually add small amounts of the flour mixture. Pinch off small pieces of dough and shape into twenty-four patties. Place on ungreased cookie sheet. Bake for twenty-five minutes. Sprinkle extra sugar and cinnamon over warm cookies.

the chief local officials of towns and villages give the *Grito* to begin the nation's birthday celebration. Suddenly the air is filled with confetti and paper streamers and noise. Huge *castillos* explode in showers of red, white, and green. Finally, in the early hours of the morning, the crowd goes home to get a few hours of sleep before continuing the celebration the next day.

On September 16 rodeos are popular in Mexico, just as they are on July 4 in the United States. So, too, are bullfights and performances by *charros*, skillful horseback riders who perform on equally skillful horses. Both riders and horses are decorated with silver ornaments. Buttons, buckles, spurs, stirrups, harnesses, and knife and pistol handles shine as the riders proudly show off the ability of their mounts.

Naturally, feasting is an important part of the independence holiday. A famous dish created especially for the Mexican Independence Day is *chiles en nogadas. Nogada* is a sauce of pounded walnuts and spice, and the dish contains green chilis, white cream, and red pomegranate seeds—the colors of the Mexican flag.

Banners and posters showing Father Hidalgo's picture are carried in parades and displayed at entertainments such as bullfights. Speeches are made to recall the priest's martyrdom for his country. And his statues are draped with garlands of flowers.

OTHER NATIONAL DAYS Columbus Day, October 12, is an important national holiday in Mexico, just as it is in the United States. But for Mexicans it has a special meaning and a special name. They call Columbus Day the Día de La Raza (Day of the Race) because it is considered the beginning of the blending of Spanish and Indian people to form a new race in Mexico.

Although Christopher Columbus was Italian, he sailed under the flag of Spain to the New World. And he is recognized by Mexico for bringing the Spanish language and Spanish customs to America. Statues of Columbus can be seen in almost every town of any size in Mexico. On October 12 they are hung with flower garlands, and there are fiestas that include colorful parades, speeches, feasting, and fireworks to honor Columbus.

A hundred years after Father Hidalgo rang his church bell and uttered the *Grito de Dolores* on September 16, 1810, another patriotic Mexican, Francisco Madero, began another revolution. For thirty years, Mexico had been ruled by a dictator named Porfirio Díaz. He ignored the reform laws. Under his rule the rich people grew richer and the poor people grew even poorer and more hopeless.

Madero called for a revolt against Díaz by all Mexicans on November 20, 1910. The people answered his call, and many of Díaz's own troops joined the rebels. Díaz had to resign and go into hiding. But the revolution turned out to be bloodier and longer than anyone could have imagined. It took ten years of terrible bloodshed before the country was again at peace under a stable government.

Today the beginning of that long revolution is remembered on November 20 with a nationwide fiesta. In Mexico City the Anniversary of the Revolution is celebrated with a huge parade of athletes. Whole soccer, baseball, football, and basketball teams plus individual boxers, wrestlers, and tennis players march. Children in their school gym uniforms also join in.

The high point of the parade for the cheering crowds that line the streets is the passing of the *charros*. Wearing their fancy riding costumes studded with silver decorations, the *charros* proudly ride their prancing horses, which are also magnificently arrayed with silver.

Smaller towns and villages hold smaller parades on November 20. But in each one there is as elaborate a fiesta as the people can afford. After the parading and the eating and the drinking and the dancing, there are sure to be brilliant fireworks displays in remembrance of the start of the revolution that marked a turning point in Mexican history.

Fiestas Galore

Besides the religious and patriotic fiestas already described, Mexicans celebrate many others all year round. Some are observed throughout the country, others are strictly regional or local. Each town or village honors its special patron saint (or saints) or its own special political leader or its special product.

There are so many fiestas in Mexico that when the government tourist office tried to list them all, it had to publish a book of nearly two hundred pages! The numbers become endless if you add all the private fiestas to celebrate birthdays, weddings, baptisms, first communions, and confirmations. No two fiestas, however, are ever quite alike, and that is part of their charm.

For the Mexicans the year fittingly begins with a fiesta. New Year's Day is a national holiday in Mexico, and it is a time for merrymaking and for agricultural and livestock fairs. Businesses and schools are closed, and newly elected officials are sworn into office.

At New Year's fiestas, vendors gather on plazas to offer handcrafted items such as pottery, woven baskets, and good-luck charms for the new year. Balloon artists are especially popular at New Year's fiestas. They make all kinds of fantastic people and animals by twisting together balloons of different shapes and sizes. The balloon artists are colorful additions to the fiestas as they stroll along holding dozens of balloon creations that dance on strings high over the heads of the crowd.

In Mexico, as in countries all over the world, New Year's Eve is a time to think back over the past and to try to look forward into the future. In Mitla, in the state of Oaxaca, Zapotec Indians celebrate New Year's Eve, which they call "Wishing Night," with bonfires. They keep all-night vigils around the bonfires.

Some Mexican families still keep the old Spanish custom of eating twelve grapes or twelve raisins on the twelve strokes of midnight for good luck in each of the twelve months to come. In Mexico's cities, towns, and villages, as midnight strikes on New Year's Eve, whistles, horns, church bells, and fireworks explosions welcome in the new year.

In some parts of Mexico an unusual and amusing dance is performed on New Year's Day. The *Danza de Los Viejitos* (Dance of the Little Old Men) is one of the oldest dances in the country. Young men are made up to look like wrinkled, toothless old men. They hobble out on sticks and stumble around as if they can hardly move.

Suddenly they straighten up and leap and jump around full of pep. But after a few minutes the dancers collapse and become weak old men—until another spurt of energy strikes them. The audience screams with laughter as they again collapse and rub their aching backs and finally hobble off the dance floor.

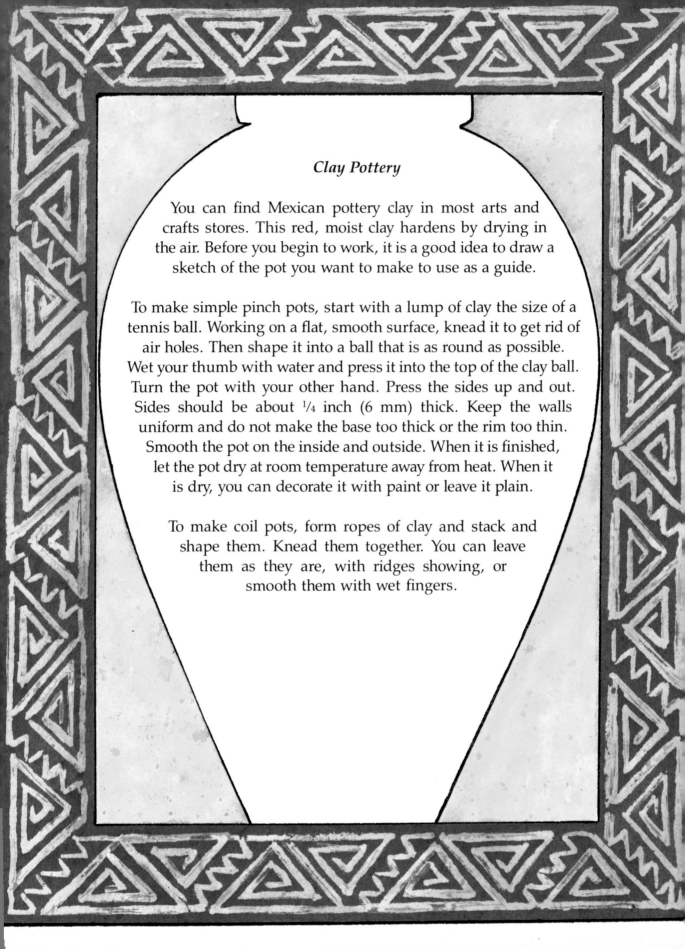

Clay Pottery

You can find Mexican pottery clay in most arts and crafts stores. This red, moist clay hardens by drying in the air. Before you begin to work, it is a good idea to draw a sketch of the pot you want to make to use as a guide.

To make simple pinch pots, start with a lump of clay the size of a tennis ball. Working on a flat, smooth surface, knead it to get rid of air holes. Then shape it into a ball that is as round as possible. Wet your thumb with water and press it into the top of the clay ball. Turn the pot with your other hand. Press the sides up and out. Sides should be about ¼ inch (6 mm) thick. Keep the walls uniform and do not make the base too thick or the rim too thin. Smooth the pot on the inside and outside. When it is finished, let the pot dry at room temperature away from heat. When it is dry, you can decorate it with paint or leave it plain.

To make coil pots, form ropes of clay and stack and shape them. Knead them together. You can leave them as they are, with ridges showing, or smooth them with wet fingers.

SPRING AND SUMMER In the springtime, many areas have fiestas that feature flowers and fruit. From March 10 to 21, Irapuato, the strawberry capital of Mexico, holds an annual Strawberry Fair and Agricultural, Livestock, Industrial and Handicrafts Exposition. A festival queen is crowned and there are dances, bullfights, and fireworks to add to the fun.

The Spring Fair of San Marcos in Aguascalientes, which runs from April 25 through May 5, is one of Mexico's biggest and liveliest fiestas. It features *matachin* dancers, mariachi bands, and bullfights.

Mexico's Labor Day on May 1 is a national holiday. Workers parade through the streets of most towns. And Mother's Day on May 10 is a fixed date on which all mothers and grandmothers are honored. June 1 is a good day to be in a seaport town to watch regattas and parades of decorated ships saluting Navy Day. The popular resort town of Acapulco holds one of the most colorful celebrations on this day when Mexican naval heroes are remembered.

All during July, the Flower Festival of Our Lady of Carmen is celebrated in various ways across Mexico. There are fairs, bullfights, fireworks, and sporting competitions, including a fishing tournament. Mexico's national sport, *fútbol* (soccer), is sure to be played in Mexico City and other towns. On July 16 special celebrations are held to honor Our Lady of Carmen, and on this date *conchero* (shell) dancers perform in the atrium (open courtyard) of the cathedral in Mexico City.

In late July there is the Feast of Santiago, which features *charreadas*, Mexican-style rodeos. These rodeos are more stylized than the ones we are used to in the United States. The riders give displays of fancy horsemanship.

Also in July are festivals that feature fascinating ancient Indian and Spanish dances. The *Jarabe Tapatío* ("Mexican Hat Dance") is the national dance of Mexico. Male dancers wear the *charro* costume, and the women wear brightly colored full skirts that whirl about them as they move. A courting scene between a young man and a young woman is acted out as they dance with quick, hopping steps around the man's big sombrero (hat).

"The Moors and the Christians" is a popular dance that goes far back into Spanish history. Masked dancers carrying wooden swords reenact battles of the Crusades. Other Spanish dances include the use of castanets and finger snapping plus vigorous heel and toe stamping. The fast, sturdy beat of the music is catching. Audiences at fiestas soon get caught up in it and shout and clap and snap their fingers as an accompaniment.

Popular Indian fiesta dances include the "Feather Dance" or "Plume Dance," in which the costumes represent the Quetzal bird. The modern version is just like the ancient one, which honored the god of music, song, dance, and of the air. The costume features a spectacular headpiece, covered with bright feathers and sparkling with mirrors set into patterns.

FALL AND WINTER San Miguel (St. Michael's) Day, September 29, is another good example of a regional fiesta. Every town or village with Miguel in its name celebrates. The most famous of these fiestas is in the small colonial town of San Miguel de Allende, where the holiday stretches to include the whole weekend nearest that day. Suddenly the trees in the *zócalo* bloom with pink, purple, and orange paper roses. The buildings surrounding the square are decorated with flags and lights.

Before dawn on Saturday morning a procession carrying lanterns and banners and led by musicians marches up to the cathedral. They represent Lucifer and his band of bad angels. When they arrive at the church, they throw fireworks at it. But the church is not damaged because San Miguel protects it. So for the rest of the weekend, he is honored with a huge fiesta.

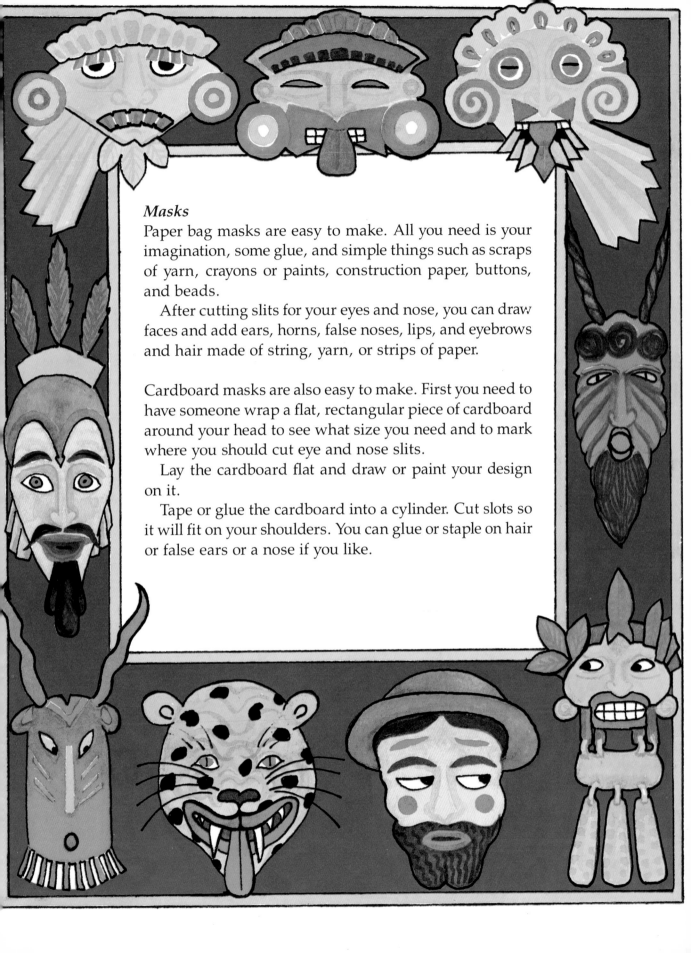

Masks

Paper bag masks are easy to make. All you need is your imagination, some glue, and simple things such as scraps of yarn, crayons or paints, construction paper, buttons, and beads.

After cutting slits for your eyes and nose, you can draw faces and add ears, horns, false noses, lips, and eyebrows and hair made of string, yarn, or strips of paper.

Cardboard masks are also easy to make. First you need to have someone wrap a flat, rectangular piece of cardboard around your head to see what size you need and to mark where you should cut eye and nose slits.

Lay the cardboard flat and draw or paint your design on it.

Tape or glue the cardboard into a cylinder. Cut slots so it will fit on your shoulders. You can glue or staple on hair or false ears or a nose if you like.

On Saturday afternoon the *conchero* dancers gather. They march into town carrying carefully built arches of flower and cactus arrangements. They place these close to the entrance of the cathedral. Then they are ready to dance. Plumes wave, capes swirl, and beads and mirrors and spangles flash as the *concheros* perform in the intricate dance patterns that tell the old, old stories handed down through countless generations.

The schoolchildren of San Miguel de Allende march in parades on Saturday and Sunday mornings, accompanied by their teachers. They are followed by bands, a fife-and-drum corps, and soldiers. There is a big fair in the marketplace with games and rides. Vendors sell oranges, ears of corn roasted over small grills, soup, tortillas, tacos, barbecued kid (young goat), and other tasty food and drink.

A good-sized crowd flocks to the bullring, not far from the market. Mexican fighting bulls were brought to Mexico from Spain within a few years of the conquest. Bullfighting has remained a popular sport since then. The *corrida de toros*, or bullfight, begins with a colorful parade. Usually each matador fights two bulls in an afternoon. The watchers know a lot about each move the matador makes. Shouts of *"Ole!"* ("Bravo!") fill the air with every good pass he makes. However, if he does not take any risks and gives an unexciting performance, they are just as quick to hiss him.

Like all good fiestas, this one ends in an explosion of noise and color. Rockets and *castillos* (castle fireworks) send volley after volley of sound and cascades of color that brighten the plaza and the upturned faces of the watchers with light. A final burst falls in a golden shower over the cathedral. Darkness follows, and it is time for the tired celebrators to return home.

One of the most unusual fiestas in all of Mexico happens in Oaxaca on December 23, the Night of the Radishes. On this

Guacamole

Guacamole is a very popular salad in Mexico. It is made from avocados, a pulpy green pear-shaped fruit that grows on a tropical tree.

Ingredients
 2 avocados
½ small white onion
 2 tomatoes
 1 jalapeño pepper (optional)
 2 tablespoons (30 ml) lemon juice
 2 to 3 sprigs fresh cilantro (coriander) (optional)
    salt and pepper

Equipment
chopping board
chopping knife
fork
measuring spoon
medium mixing bowl
plastic wrap or foil

How to make
Peel avocados and mash with fork. Put in bowl. Chop onion, cilantro, and pepper finely. Peel tomatoes and chop finely. Add all chopped ingredients to bowl. Add lemon juice and salt and pepper to taste. Mix well. If you're not serving right away, cover bowl tightly with plastic wrap or foil. (This helps keep salad from discoloring.) Then refrigerate. Serve in bowl with corn chips on the side to dip into the salad. This recipe serves six people.

day booths are set up along one side of the *zócalo*. Here Indians from the surrounding mountains display their radish creations. Some of these are weird, some are funny, and some are truly works of art. The radishes come in different sizes and shapes. Small smooth red radishes, huge hairy black radishes, and elongated white radishes are carved to look like animals, people, and objects.

At one Radish Fiesta there was a radish figure of Cuban leader Fidel Castro complete with his beard. Also featured was a shark with toothpick teeth, as well as a miniature circus of radish animals—elephants, seals balancing balls, and bareback riders on prancing radish horses. At nightfall judges study the displays and award prizes for the funniest or most imaginative creations. Each year huge crowds come to see the radish artwork.

As we have seen, it is impossible to say just how many fiestas there are in Mexico. It is also impossible to know how much time and money are devoted to them. The national, regional, patriotic, religious, trade, and local fiestas mentioned in this book are only a fraction of the total number.

Are these fiestas worth all the expense and effort? For the millions of Mexicans for whom they are a release from the daily grind and a chance to connect with God, country, family, friends, and neighbors, the answer would certainly be a resounding *"sí!"*

Glossary

buñuelo (boon-NYWAY-loh): Mexican doughnut

calenda (kah-LEHN-dah): religious procession

calendula (kah-LEHN-duh-lah): marigold; special flower of the dead

castillo (kahs-TEE-yoh): castle; elaborate fireworks structure

chalupa (chah-LOO-pah): open-face fried tortilla with beans, tomatoes, shredded lettuce, and grated cheese

charreada (chah-reh-AH-dah): Mexican-style rodeo

charro (CHAH-roh): Mexican horseman or cowboy

chile rellenos (CHEE-lay ray-YAHN-nohs): green chili peppers filled with cheese and dipped in batter before baking

chiles en nogadas (CHEE-lays en noh-GAH-dahs): famous red, white, and green dish created for Mexican Independence Day

china poblana (CHEE-nah poh-BLAH-nah): colorful Mexican costume

conchero (kohn-CHAY-roh): dance group that performs to the accompaniment of guitars made from shells (*conchas*) of armadillos

empanada (em-pah-NAH-dah): turnover filled with sweet potato, pumpkin, or meat filling

enchilada (ehn-chee-LAH-dah): rolled tortilla with a meat, cheese, or chicken and chili pepper stuffing

frijoles (free-HOH-lehs): beans

Hidalgo (ee-DAHL-goh), *Father Miguel* (1753–1811): leader of Mexican revolution against Spain

Huichols (WHEE-chols): Indians who live in state of Jalisco in central Mexico and cling to old customs and rituals

Juárez (HWA-ras), *Benito* (1806–1872): president of Mexico (1861–65, 1867–72)

machete (mah-CHAY-tay): large heavy knife

mariachi (mah-ree-ACH-chee): wandering street band. A typical mariachi group has six to eight musicians: a singer-leader, two horn players, two violin players, two guitarists, and one bass player

matachines (mah-tah-CHEE-nays) (sing. *matachin*): group of Indian dancers licensed by the government, dedicated to serving the Virgin of Guadalupe

matador (mah-tah-DOOR): man appointed to kill bull in bullfights

mestizo (mez-TEE-soh): Mexican of Spanish and Indian ancestry

Montezuma II (mon-teh-ZOO-mah) (also Moctezuma) (1466–1520): last Aztec emperor (1502–1520) of Mexico

mulitos (moo-LEE-tohs): little mules

Nacimiento (nah-see-MEEYEN-toh): manger scene

Noche Buena (no-chay-BWAY-na): Christmas Eve

Oaxaca (wah-HAH-kah): city in South Mexico famous for elaborate fiestas

pan de los muertos (pahn-deh-los-MWAIR-tohs): special bread for the Day of the Dead fiesta

piñata (pee-NYAH-tah): decorated form filled with candy and small gifts

posada (poh-SAH-dah): inn, shelter; the name *Posada* also is given to the reenactment of Mary and Joseph's search for shelter

pozole (poh-SOH-lay): stew or thick soup made with pork, hominy, and chilies

quesadilla (kay-sah-DEE-yah): tortilla baked with cheese, which is sometimes mixed into the dough

Quetzalcoatl (kayt-sahl-KOH-atl): the Plumed Serpent, an Aztec god

rebozo (ray-BOH-soh): shawl

refresco (ray-FRES-coh): native soft drink; fruit juice diluted with water and sweetened with honey or sugar

serape (seh-RAH-pay): blanket; sometimes worn as a cloak by Mexican Indians

Tenochtitlán (teh-noch-tee-TLAN): Aztec city where Mexico City is today

torero (tor-REH-roh): bullfighter

tortilla (tor-TEE-yah): flat, round pancakelike bread made of corn or flour

voladores (voh-lah-DOOR-rays): flying dancers called "birdmen"

zócalo (SOH-kah-loh): public square, plaza

A Calendar of Mexican Fiestas

SOME OF THE MOST IMPORTANT AND POPULAR FIESTAS

January 1	New Year's Day—major celebrations and fairs in many states.
January 6	Day of the Three Kings—Three Kings bring gifts to Mexican children.
January 17	Day of St. Anthony—blessing of household animals and livestock.
February 2–8	Candlemas Day—blessing of seeds and candles.
February 5	Constitution Day—parades and speeches.
February 24	Flag Day—commemorates origin of Mexican flag in 1821.
February–March	Carnival throughout Mexico.
Palm Sunday	Blessing of the Palms.
Holy Week	Religious dramas throughout week; Passion plays; in San Miguel de Allende altars decorated with flowers and fruit set up in front of private homes.
Holy Saturday	Large paper effigies (likenesses) of Judas, politicians, skeletons, devils strung with firecrackers and set on fire.
Easter	Church ceremonies.
March 19	Day of San José—many towns of this name hold fiestas.

March 21	Birthday of Benito Juárez and Day of the Indian Child.
April 25–May 5	Huge San Marcos Fair in Aguascalientes; famous celebration held for over three centuries to celebrate city's founding.
May 1	Labor Day—workers' parades.
May 5	Cinco de Mayo—commemorates defeat of French at Puebla in 1862.
May 10	Mother's Day.
June	Feast of Corpus Christi (eight weeks and four days after Easter)—Spectacular performances by the *voladores* (flying dancers) called "birdmen" at Papantla and other cities. In Mexico City, children dressed in traditional costumes carry baskets filled with fruit and vegetables to cathedral as token tithings (church taxes). Straw mules are popular gifts.
June 1	Navy Day—observed in Mexican seaports.
June 24	St. John the Baptist's Day—popular national holiday when anyone may get an unexpected "baptism" by being pushed into a pool or fountain or by having water thrown on him or her.
July	Dance festival in Oaxaca—attended by Indians in varied, colorful costumes; folk dances including the Zancudos (long-legged wading birds) performed on stilts.
July (entire month)	Feast of Our Lady of Carmen—flower festival with celebrations on 16th or nearest Sunday.
Late July	Feast of Santiago—national holiday featuring *charreadas* (Mexican-style rodeos).
August 15	Feast of the Assumption of the Blessed Virgin Mary—celebrated nationwide; includes running of the bulls and decorating of church doors with flowers.
September 16	Independence Day—special ceremonies in all state capitals; biggest celebrations in Mexico City.
September 29	San Miguel Day—honors St. Michael, patron saint of all towns with San Miguel in their names. Big carnival in San Miguel de Allende on nearest weekend.

October	October festivals—Month of cultural and sporting events with floats, costumed merrymakers, dancers, concerts, shows, fairs, and sporting competitions in Guadalajara.
October 12	Columbus Day (Day of the Race)—honors Columbus and commemorates blending of Indian and Spanish races to form Mexican people.
October–November	International Cervantes Festival—cultural event in Guanajuato with performances by world-famous singers, dancers, musicians, and actors.
November 1–2	All Saints' and All Souls' Day (Day of the Dead)—important festival for remembering the dead throughout Mexico.
November 20	Anniversary of the Mexican Revolution of 1910—national holiday with huge parade of athletes in Mexico City.
November–December	National Silver Fair—annual event in Taxco, where silver is displayed and sold.
December 12	Feast Day of the Virgin of Guadalupe—important religious festival. Mexico's patron saint is honored with processions and folk dances throughout the country. Hundreds of thousands of pilgrims come to worship at her shrine on the outskirts of Mexico City.
December 16–24	Posadas—nine days of traditional religious celebrations with processions, parades, and elaborate fireworks.
December 25	Christmas—church services and family feasts.
December 31	New Year's Eve—midnight masses and New Year's parties.

For Further Reading

Casagrande, Louis B., and Johnson, Sylvia A. *Focus on Mexico*. Minneapolis: Lerner Publications, 1986.

Fisher, Leonard Everett. *Pyramid of the Sun/Pyramid of the Moon*. New York: Macmillan, 1988.

Hancock, Ralph. *Mexico*. New York: Macmillan, 1964.

Ikuhara, Yoshiyuki. *Children of the World/Mexico*. Milwaukee: Gareth Stevens Publishing, 1987.

Marcus, Rebecca B., and Marcus, Judith. *Fiesta Time in Mexico*. Champaign, Ill.: Garrard Publishing, 1974.

Moran, Tom. *A Family in Mexico*. Minneapolis: Lerner Publications, 1987.

Nevins, Albert J. *Away to Mexico*. New York: Dodd, Mead, 1966.

Perl, Lila. *Mexico/Crucible of the Americas*. New York: William Morrow, 1978.

Stein, R. Conrad. *Mexico* (Enchantment of the World series). Chicago: Childrens Press, 1984.

Syme, Ronald. *Juárez/The Founder of Modern Mexico*. New York: William Morrow, 1972.

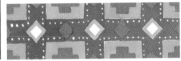

Index

[63]